This book is based on the author's successful lecture series, "Astonish the World, Tell the Simple Truth." Examples of comments received:

"The best talk I ever heard regarding all aspects of our human experience, past, present, and future. A joy! Ingenious!"
—Mary E. May, Sun City Center, Florida

"This was the clearest presentation of reality that I ever heard. It could form the basis for a new belief system."
—Ernest Kerr, South Bend, Indiana

"I've attended lectures by the most highly regarded teachers. None gave more usable and inspiring information than you did. An awe-inspiring, brilliant presentation! How I wish everyone could be in attendance."
—Fred Burrous, Bradenton Beach, Florida

"He is a born teacher."
—Fred Ryersbach, M.D., Sarasota, Florida

"An awesome presentation. Personable, intellectual, and profoundly understandable, Simonetta has a brilliant and organized mind . . . a gift for sure . . . that he uses to assist the evolution of humankind."
—The Reverend Vinita Anne Watkins, San Diego, California

"Simonetta has an incredible ability to coalesce information and articulate it."
—Robert O. Ball, Bradenton, Florida

"I was fascinated with your thought-provoking presentation. The concept of your ingenious 'three commandments,' based on common sense logic, gives a hint for humanity's 'raison d'etre' and a simple path to the ultimate truth."
—Frank Vona, Brantford, Ontario, Canada

". . . master of various degrees and a concise, courageous speaker. Your address was explosive and your memory-quotient awesome."

—Received anonymously, Sarasota, Florida

Typical readers' comments:

"I cannot adequately express my admiration for your erudition and the lucidity of your writing. The content is really inspirational and compares to that of *Conversations with God*."

—Sid Kobernick, M.D., Sarasota, Florida

"I've been trying to understand this all my life; you have really figured it out."

—Charles Thompson, Sun City Center, Florida

". . . marvelous, succinct, right on target, the right message at the right time."

—Jean Mitchell, Ph.D., Annapolis, Maryland

"You have helped me to see the purpose of life for which I had been looking for many, many years."

—David Croud, Cambridge, Massachusetts

"This is it!"

—Robert Beckwith, biologist, Boise, Idaho

". . . elegant, lean and clear writing. The book is altogether beautifully done."

—Cher Gilmore, Canton, GA

". . . the simplest, most concise, most perfect definition of Democracy I ever heard or read . . . I'm taken with your ability to take complex issues and make the message and solutions so simple and elegant."

—David Mitchell, Annapolis, Maryland

"Liberating!"

—Mary Allmann, Wausau, Wisconsin

SEVEN WORDS THAT CAN CHANGE THE WORLD

OTHER BOOKS BY

Joseph R. Simonetta

The Heroes Are Us:
A Call to Rescue Our World

Russell, Alexandra, and John:
A Story of Personal and Planetary Change

The Book of Pithies, Volume I

The Book of Pithies, Volume II

SEVEN WORDS THAT CAN CHANGE THE WORLD

a new understanding of sacredness

Joseph R. Simonetta

WALSCH
BOOKS

an imprint of
HAMPTON ROADS
PUBLISHING COMPANY, INC.
www.hrpub.com

Cover design by Marjoram Productions

Hampton Roads Publishing Company, Inc.
1125 Stoney Ridge Road
Charlottesville, VA 22902

434-296-2772
fax: 434-296-5096
e-mail: hrpc@hrpub.com
www.hrpub.com

If you are unable to order this book from your local
bookseller, you may order directly from the publisher.
Call 1-800-766-8009, toll-free.

Library of Congress Catalog Card Number: 2001092125
ISBN 1-57174-295-6

10 9 8 7 6 5 4 3 2 1

Printed on acid-free paper in Canada

This book is dedicated to a dear friend, the late Dr. Fred Ryersbach (1910–1999). A faithful husband and father, caring physician, classical pianist, voracious reader and conversationalist, avid chess player, patron of the arts, intellectual, and lifetime tennis player and athlete, Fred was a kind and brilliant man who made us think harder.

CONTENTS

PART I: INTRODUCTION / 1

PART II: THE PROBLEM / 9

PART III: THE SOLUTION / 37

ACKNOWLEDGEMENTS

I would like to acknowledge the contribution of Dr. Richard Fern of Yale Divinity School for his support and encouragement when I was a student at Yale. And while I was at Harvard, thank you to Dr. Ted Hiebert, Dr. Timothy C. Weiskel and Dr. Gordon D. Kaufman, all of Harvard Divinity School, for their candor and willingness to challenge conventionality. Thank you to Dr. Edward O. Wilson for his evolutionary biology class at Harvard and for his overall brilliance. Thank you to Rev. Edwin Lynn, minister of North Shore Unitarian Universalist Church, Danvers, Massachusetts, and advisor and instructor at Harvard Divinity School, for his encouragement. A special thank you to Dr. Elmer Ruhnke for his editing assistance with an earlier version of this book.

Ernie Kerr played a major role in the development of this book. I first met Ernie at one of my speaking engagements. We happened to sit next to each other. Before I even gave my address, Ernie challenged me with insightful theological questions. After my talk, he said to me, "That was the clearest presentation of reality I have ever heard. It could form the basis for a new belief system. How can I help you?" He has since helped in many ways including his excellent editing assistance on this book. His keen intellect, friendship, and support have been invaluable.

PREFACE

When I was a candidate for Congress from Pennsylvania's 15th Congressional District after I won my party's nomination in the 1986 primary election, a professor from Lehigh University said to me, "You know, you are liable to win this election; you're trying something different. You're telling the truth." As it turned out, the fifth-term incumbent congressman whom I challenged and who outspent me nine to one (I refused to seek or accept PAC money) won in the general election. I received forty-three percent of the vote, more than any previous challenger. I worked hard for and achieved the name recognition that would have enabled me to launch another challenge two years later. I decided not to do that.

From my seventeen-month, nonstop political campaign, I got a good taste of the world of politics. The answers to our problems can never come from that battleground of adversarial self-interest groups. There are larger issues and realities that first must be understood and resolved. Then the political process can be influenced for the benefit of the common good. The "simple truths" in this book address those larger issues and realities.

FOREWORD

Well, here it is. The Formula. The Answer. The Way.

Of course, everyone has The Formula, The Answer, The Way. This is not the private domain of gurus on mountaintops or teachers in temples. The guru in your heart knows The Formula. The teacher in the temple of your being has The Answer. And your soul itself *is* The Way. Still, it is nice to have it articulated so brilliantly, so fluently, so directly and unambiguously as we see it here.

When I first read this material I found myself turning the corner of a page every time I came across something that I knew I wanted to slip into my talks. I give little talks around the world on life, the meaning of existence, and the way to have it all make sense, and as I was reading Joe Simonetta's words I thought, "Wow. I can use this as a reference. This is really good."

But by the time I got finished reading I had turned down nearly every other page. I thought, "My God, I'm going to have to memorize this man's entire book."

I knew then that I had to make sure I played my role in getting it to a larger audience, because I thought, "Gosh, if I'm responding to this book in this way, so will other people."

And I was right. Every other person to whom I've shown this material has said, basically, what I said when I put it down. Which was: "Whoa. What a powerful book. Really remarkable. Elegant simplicity."

This is a totally empowering piece of writing. Do not be misled by its small size. It is just as meaningful (perhaps more so) than any five- or six-hundred-page book I have ever read. If you are looking to help change our planet, if you are wishing to change your own life, you have just given yourself the most practical tools you will ever have. With these simple tools you will say, "I can *do* this. This is something *I can do.*"

Tampa, Florida, radio personality Joel Chudnow refers to the little gem of a book that you are now holding as "a thousand-page book in a hundred pages." I like that. That pretty much says it.

There are three rules of life listed here. Three rules, seven words. Those seven words can heal the world. So I didn't have to memorize Joe's entire book after all. I only had to remember three rules, seven words.

Here they are. Seven words. A simple mantra that will work. A little secret that will renew your enthusiasm for life.

Here it is. The Formula. The Answer. The Way.

One formula. One answer. One way. There are others, of course. We all know that. There is more than one path to paradise. But this path is so *simple*. So *practical*. So *easy*. It allows us to come to a new understanding of sacredness without all the trappings of some other approaches—without years of study and meditation, without rituals to perform and masters to follow, without classes or workshops or seminars, without, well, much effort at all. Which is how it should be, it has always seemed to me. Truth should be a simple thing.

So here it is. The Simple Truth.

Enjoy.

And pass it on.

Neale Donald Walsch

PART 1

INTRODUCTION

As a child, I wondered,
"Why do we create so many problems?"

Allow me to relate to you the nature of my background. It will help you understand how I arrived at the conclusions you will find in this book. Please grant me this indulgence.

As a child, I was disturbed by the insensitive and unkind ways we humans treat each other. I recognized that the pattern was wrong and unsustainable. "Why do we create so many problems?" I wondered. "Life need not be this difficult," I thought. At that young age, I could not understand much beyond my instinct that something was wrong. Ahead were many roads for me to travel and much to learn.

As I experienced and observed life as a young man and later as an adult, I continued to be troubled deeply by cruel and destructive behavior that I witnessed over and over. I was disturbed that our world is thick with suffering, inequity, injustice, and exploitation. I was haunted without relief by how we destroy each other, our environment, and even our own bodies and minds. I wondered how we could live amidst abundance yet simultaneously exist in a sea of anxiety, fear, insecurity, greed, and self-centeredness.

I had a desperate need to understand. My inherent nature, contemplative and proactive, drove me into the classrooms of our world. My curiosity and sense of adventure propelled me. My abilities and discipline enabled and sustained me. Circumstances and serendipity allowed me. I became, and I am to this day, a student of life.

In my travels and experiences, I was aware of my motion but not my destination. The latter I knew to be distant. It would reveal itself only after an arduous journey, just as a great mountain yields its summit only after one conquers its lesser peaks. Victories and defeats nourished and thrashed me. I forged on in search of the common but elusive thread that weaves through and binds all relationships. I immersed myself in rich learning experiences in a broad range of seemingly unrelated fields. I feel as if I have lived numerous lifetimes.

Over time, external forms began to dissolve into a transparency that revealed glimpses of the underlying foundation that girds our existence. Clarity emerged that liberated me from much of the cultural programming to which we are subjected relentlessly. I began to see and understand the cause and effect relationships of life. Once clear, I was able to ask and answer some fundamental questions. I examined our religious belief systems because, for many of us, they color our observations and form the basis for our decisions that result in our actions. I searched to discover that which is sacred. While all religions claim to have sacred qualities, I was determined to identify those things, in this life, that are truly sacred.

Drawing on my life's experiences, and study, and still more experiences as a student at Harvard and Yale Divinity Schools, I finally found what I was after. It is a way of relating that is not arbitrary but imperative. It addresses the reality that everything in our world is related and that the proper manner of these relationships must be understood and practiced if we are to survive as a species. This manner of relating is characterized by qualities that nourish and sustain the relationships of life, as opposed to those that damage and destroy them. It may be that which Lao Tzu refers to in the Tao Te Ching (The Way of Life) written twenty-six hundred years ago. The answers are simple, elegant really, but elusive. They have to do with what I refer to as the foundational relationships of life, sacred relationships. Out of and within these, all relationships and endeavors follow and occur. As you read on, you will understand.

The odyssey of my life that propelled me

through a labyrinth of rich educational experiences convinces me that we humans must find a new track on which to travel. It is evident that there is a need for a belief system more relevant to the complex and increasingly sophisticated age in which we live, a belief system with the potential to achieve universal acceptance. A belief system responsive to the problems of our time and capable of drawing people everywhere together. Of most importance, a belief system that can reduce ignorance and suffering and expand knowledge and justice. I concluded, after I spoke with many others, that there are countless people—an ever-growing number—who seek such a belief system.

While there are many who are satisfied with their present belief systems, there are at least as many who are not. Curious to know what my fellow divinity students at Harvard thought about the need for a new belief system, I took a formal written survey of their opinions. Most, I found, were dissatisfied and felt a need for revisions to their belief systems or desired an entirely new one that would address current issues with current knowledge.

Within the diverse survey responses of my fellow students were unifying themes. There was a strong call for a universal belief system that would be acceptable to everyone and that would honor the dignity of each person. There was an abiding respect for diversity that allows for and encourages both individuality and blending within the reality of our interdependence. There was a desire for a non-patriarchal belief system and an equitable distribution of power. There was a desire for a belief system that is more contemporary and more relevant to life in this world. There was a passion for social change and the elimination of inequities. There was a wish that people around the world would develop a global sense of community that transcends the limited notion of nation-states, because we all have fundamental needs in common. There was a call for truth and knowledge. Resonating throughout the responses was a clarion call for recognition of the sacredness of the natural world, and that the care and respect for planet Earth is a "sacred" duty.

I was encouraged by the results of that survey. For many years, I spent countless hours sifting through volumes of information in hallowed university halls and the not-so-hallowed streets of many cities searching for answers. Now, I discovered that the answers I found and the belief system to which those answers led me addressed all of the concerns that the survey revealed, and more. Let me take you through an overview of what I perceive to be our problem. Following that is the architecture—the design and structure—of the solution.

PART II

THE PROBLEM

"Technological societies know how to create material wealth, but their ultimate success will depend on their ability to formulate a postindustrial humanistic culture. The shift from obsession with quantitative growth to the search for a better life will not be possible without radical changes in attitudes."

Rene Dubos, *Celebrations of Life*

MEANS WITHOUT GOALS

Many of us are troubled by much of what we observe and experience in life. Increasing numbers of us seek meaning and purpose in an often impersonal, materialistic, and adversarial world. We share a growing conviction that reconciliation among people, nations, races, and diverse political, economic, and religious ideologies is unattainable and maybe even impossible. It is perplexing and disturbing.

In a world dominated by fear and greed, we exploit each other and ravage our environment. In our passion to consume and accumulate, we are increasingly competitive, confrontational, and self-centered. We take our pleasures but do not replenish. We deplete and exhaust the land, abuse our bodies, and violate our spirit. We create unsustainable imbalances.

We experience and exhibit contradictions that cause confusion and anxiety. We are capable of infinite compassion and the cruelest brutalities. We create extraordinary beauty and unimaginable horror. We are sustained by the fruits of our labor while we destroy the environment from which we derive our bounty. We celebrate our uniqueness, deny others theirs, and profess our superiority.

We've been graced with abundance yet many are in great need. We have been given every freedom, yet to many freedom is denied. Many of us who have every need fulfilled create insatiable wants. We have every means to resolve our problems, yet they persist.

We exhibit a vengeance for getting ahead but sense we are somehow falling behind in some intangible way. *The Times* of London columnist Bernard Levin writes of countries that are "full of people who have all the material comforts they desire, yet lead lives of quiet desperation, understanding nothing but the fact that there is a hole inside of them and that however much food and drink they pour into it, however many cars and television sets they stuff it with . . . it aches."

"We spend more, but have less; we buy more, but enjoy it less. We have bigger houses and smaller families; more conveniences, but less time; we have more degrees, but less sense; more knowledge, but less judgment; more experts, but more problems; more medicine, but less wellness. We've added years to life, not life to years."

Anonymous

Results of surveys taken in the United States, Western Europe, and Japan to determine the effects of technological progress and the steadily rising standard of living on human health and happiness were essentially the same in all the wealthy industrial nations. While many believed that knowledge and the state of health had improved, a large majority felt that inner happiness and peace of mind had diminished. Something is fundamentally wrong.

In stark contrast to our measurable achievements, a quality of life for which we long remains distressingly beyond our reach. It is the essence, the very nectar of existence that remains stubbornly elusive. It is a quality of life that can provide us with mental and physical well-being and lead to fewer troubled relationships. It is the unfulfilled half of our potential of which our higher selves are mindful. It lies dormant, awaiting release and expression like a genie trapped in a bottle.

World-renowned scientist, humanist, and Pulitzer Prize-winning author Rene Dubos writes, "Technological societies know how to create material wealth, but their ultimate success will depend on their ability to formulate a postindustrial humanistic culture. The shift from obsession with quantitative growth to the search for a better life will not be possible without radical changes in attitudes. The Industrial Revolution placed a premium on the kind of intelligence best suited to the invention of manufactured articles, as well as to their production and distribution on a large scale. In contrast, a humanistic society would prize more highly skills facilitating better human relationships and more creative interplay between humankind, nature, and technology."

Where once our abundance of natural resources counterbalanced our limited vision, today we find ourselves in a new arena. Now the limitations of our resources and the extraordinary growth of our population must be compensated for by an expansion of our vision. Similarly, we find that we can no longer engage in our primitive form of conflict resolution, warfare, lest we risk our very existence. We have neither the resources nor the space to repeat the mistakes of our past. To do so would be to exhibit an archaic mentality likely to return a few survivors to an archaic time.

Expressing his concern for what he considers to be a central problem of modern civilization, Dubos notes that "science and technology provide us with the means to create almost anything we want, but the development of *means* without worthwhile *goals* generates at best a dreary life and may, at worst, lead to tragedy." A stark example is the discovery of nuclear fission, which was first used to make tens of thousands of thermonuclear warheads.

Today, we stand on the threshold of comprehending the oneness and the interlocking whole of which we are a part. It informs us that life is not assured—it is dependent upon the interrelationships by which it is sustained. Because these interrelationships are as fundamental as natural laws, our problems are like those we might suffer by arrogantly defying the law of gravity. An understanding of the significance of our connectedness and interdependence can serve as a powerful change agent. It goes to the philosophical heart of our decision making process.

Attitudes among individuals and institutions must change to recognize the balance in life and the sacredness of mutually beneficial life forms. We are connected. Life is fragile. This understanding is the prerequisite to the next step on our evolutionary journey. Given the complexity of our world, it is a giant step on a continually arduous journey.

Our planet, always evolving, is divided into some 190 ever-changing sovereign nations with people speaking more than 6,000 different languages. In each nation a staggering mix of political, economic, cultural, and social factors combine to produce varying qualities of life. In all these nations, individual, public-sector, and private-sector policies are typically not based on the reality of interdependence. Decisions, driven by short-term priorities, are commonly based on desires to maximize profit and to retain or gain power, all in the name of progress.

PROFIT, POWER, AND PROGRESS

What can be said of profit, power, and progress in the interrelated and interdependent reality in which we exist? What kind of people are we who allow grotesque disparities to exist between the affluent and the impoverished? How is it we allow one quarter of our human family to be doomed to a hopeless and unremitting battle for survival, while others of us are over-clothed, over-housed, and so over-fed that we have to go on special diets to lose weight?

This unequal distribution of opportunity and wealth is not accidental. Fueled by ignorance and greed, it results from economies organized to benefit the insatiable appetites of the opportunistic. Most individuals and institutions are reluctant to cede self-interest for the common good. Most countries are unwilling to think beyond sovereignty and national interests. Instead, shackled with destructive habits and short on vision, they violate relationships with each other and the environment. In doing so, they court disaster.

This is done in the name of profit, power, and progress. Consider profit: Too often it is the sole motivating force for many of us who shamelessly sacrifice human decency and environmental protection for short-term personal gains. We are driven by a surplus of greed and a lack of common sense. Profit's offspring, exploitive commercialism, fans the fires of materialism. Enormous sums are invested to convince us that we need to acquire and consume products that are often unnecessary and even harmful to ourselves and our environment. Wealth and status are glorified. Image supersedes substance. We plunder and deplete our resources, torture our ailing environment, decimate other species, and pollute our already confused minds. To what end do we invest ourselves in this fatal frivolity?

Profiteers will always clamor for more and more. Many achieve enormous wealth. For each who has much, there are countless others who have precious little. Rage and fear grow among those who experience economic insecurity. They are filled with anxiety and despair instead of a sense of community. Wealth and power, intoxicating and irresistible, blind us to these disparities and their eventual consequences. Those who exploit innocent others and destroy ecosystems can boast arrogantly of their "achievements," ignorant or in denial of their violations and the eventual consequences of their actions.

It is foolish and irresponsible to maximize profits regardless of human and environmental costs. Natural resources are not endlessly renewable and self-generating. People will tolerate only so much exploitation and repression. Eventually these violations will lead to famine, economic collapse, and political revolution.

Responsible profit taking is honorable. Those who are legitimate producers deserve to be rewarded for their earnest contributions. It is when profit taking replaces concern for others or for ecosystems that a perversity occurs whereby everyone and everything suffers. At that point, we are not evolving but devolving. Those who achieve power and allow the gap to widen between the rich and the poor promote only inequity, desperation, conflict, ecological ruin, and systemic distress. Of what value are profit, power, and progress when they violate people and other species, and destroy the conditions that sustain life? As Aldo Leopold has written, "A thing is right when it tends to preserve the integrity, stability, and beauty of the biotic community. It is wrong when it tends otherwise."

The word "progress" means moving toward a goal. However, we want to move forward on the right road. While free enterprise requires profit as an incentive to stimulate individual productivity, society requires that the welfare of the common good be acknowledged and sustained. For this, we look to our public sector for the protection of our common interests. Here too, we find the influence of private interests and the power of money and *profits* to be pervasive. Its effect on our democratic form of government is destructive.

DEMOCRACY

A prominent United States senator said recently that the influence of money in political campaign financing ". . . is nothing less than an influence-peddling scheme in which both parties compete to stay in office by selling the country to the highest bidder." In her book, *The Corruption of American Politics*, veteran Washington journalist Elizabeth Drew writes that money is drowning out decency and threatening the underpinnings of democracy itself.

This is ominous. Democracy is more than a form of government. It is a way of life, a formula for just relationships. The word "democracy" means *rule by the people*. Abraham Lincoln described this form of self-government as "government of the people, by the people, for the people," not government of some people, by some people, for some people. Democracy supports individual freedom and the fundamental dignity and equality of all persons.

Democracy, theoretically, is a form of government in which political power rests with all the people. It recognizes the intrinsic value of widespread and broad-based input. It invites the richness of diversity. Democracy says do not look only to yourself and like-minded people for answers; avail yourself of that which others have to offer, for life is diverse. Democracy says do not be rigid or inflexible; be open and adaptable, for life is dynamic and ever changing. Democracy says do not make participation exclusive; make it inclusive, for life is all encompassing. Democracy says do not gravitate to extremes; seek moderation, for life requires balance. Democracy says do not represent only those who have influence; represent all, for life demands justice. Finally, Democracy says do not tamper with this process, for it is your only hope of survival.

Democracy requires watchdogs. Always, it is under siege. This occurs when our capitalistic economic system and our democratic political system clash. Democracy calls for a government of, by, and for the people. Capitalism calls for profit. When the quest for profits plays a disproportionate role in electing candidates to public office, democracy is compromised. When office holders reward their benefactors, there is a gross violation of democracy. This legal form of institutionalized corruption defeats the spirit of democracy. When the morality of our government is corrupted, democracy disintegrates. When the government is controlled by those who seek profit above the welfare of the common good, the democratic process is rendered useless.

The democratic process represents an appreciation for life, a celebration of diversity, and an acknowledgment of our oneness. It is a process emanating from our instinct to be free, an irrepressible force. The ideals of democracy are the ideals of humanity. For democracy in our public sector and for capitalism in our private sector to work together harmoniously, we must fully understand the implications of our interdependence: the interrelationships of life, which sustain both human and ecological systems, must be honored.

Democracy is the form of government we have chosen to protect these interrelationships. Those of us who work in the public sector must understand our protective roles. The common good cannot be sacrificed for the benefit of the powerful. Those of us who labor in the free market have similar responsibilities. The first is to support, not erode, the democratic process. The second is to profit in ways that do not violate people or our environment. From these judicious uses of *power* in both sectors, we all *profit* and *progress*.

Education

We live at a time when it is necessary to evaluate our beliefs. Such an exercise is always healthy and should be ongoing. That which is antiquated and dysfunctional must be discarded. As we mature, our beliefs and priorities change. That is normal and healthy.

At one time our planet seemed like an immense and limitless place. Huge territories were unexplored and undiscovered. There was true separation between continents and peoples. Activities and consequences were confined within definable boundaries. As we grew and evolved, we began moving beyond self-defined limits, reached out, explored, connected, and interacted. We continued doing this as we became increasingly sophisticated in our abilities to travel, communicate, and trade. Today, we are, indeed, a global community.

It is evident that the fate of all living things is interconnected. We have become responsible for that fate. We are guardians of life itself.

We live at a pivotal time. We stand to either learn and benefit from our experiences and knowledge or ignore both and suffer. It is essential that we embrace a new way of relating. Whereas the first lesson of evolution was one of conflict, today's is one of kinship. We need to evolve into something more than we've been. We are called upon to make a crucial decision and choose either a world divided against itself—engaged in power struggles between its parts—or one whose richly diverse components work together for their mutual benefit. The choice is obvious.

It is important that we focus on our common interests rather than on stubborn positions that lead only to conflict. Once our interests are defined, options for mutual gain can be explored and developed. We can then address the issues that benefit everyone rather than cling to religious or political ideologies that separate us. If we hope to transcend our divisiveness, our attention must be directed at the interdependence of diverse interests. More than the outcome of any debate, we need to protect this kind of approach and process. Until we do, we are ill-fated. We no longer have the luxury of greed or ignorance. We now exist in a world community where problems anywhere have the potential to affect anyone, anywhere.

Ultimately, the problems of cities and the environment, of production and consumption, and of crime, health, and world peace are educational problems.

Our task, for which our age is well suited, is education. An enlightened public will move from alienation to community, from despair to hope, from idleness to action, from ignorance to knowledge, and from apathy to concern. People will return to the political process. As they do, politics will return to the people. Ecological balance will be integrated with human productivity, social welfare will be tempered by individual responsibility, and localism and globalism will share equal importance.

RELIGION

Is there a need for a "religion," i.e., a belief system, in all of this? The answer is a qualified "yes." We require a set of beliefs to guide us as we navigate through life. More specifically, we need a vision relevant to the complex and increasingly sophisticated age in which we live, a vision that defines what is sacred here and now in this life, not "out there" somewhere in some afterlife. A definition so clear that it changes forever our understanding of profit, power, and progress, a vision that enlightens the worlds of economics and politics and even religion itself.

Such a belief system would play a central role in our lives. It would expand knowledge and justice, and reduce ignorance and suffering. It would embody inclusiveness in the broadest sense. It would diffuse historical rivalries and contemporary adversaries engaged in ruinous relationships. It would draw us together. It would change the way we care for each other, our environment, and ourselves. It would do what many of us expect a belief system to do. It would help us achieve a healthier, more peaceful, and just world.

We exist at the threshold of a new way to understand and live life. We have evolved through the agrarian and industrial ages to a post-industrial, high-tech information age. For the first time, we have instantaneous, global communication. We are poised to disseminate the information necessary to develop a new world view: *a sacred humanistic culture* where the outlook is for the long term; where integrative approaches to problem solving are utilized; where poverty is eradicated; and where wasteful consumption patterns are eliminated. Our limitation is not technology, it is old-world thinking and ethics among leaders and followers who have vested and narrow interests in maintaining the status quo.

Much of our inability to advance stems from failure to discuss long-term interests, from unnecessary polarization, and from excessive divisions along ideological lines. In a world that abounds with astonishing diversity, one wonders how we can subscribe to the rigidity that is at the core of our problems. Our planet is small. We are not isolated from or unaffected by our neighbors as we were in our past. We are now required to satisfy ourselves as individuals *and* as members of larger communities.

We are like a body of people involved in a grand experiment that might be described in the following manner. Imagine a beautiful island resplendent with majestic mountains, lush valleys, gorgeous beaches, clean air, sparkling waters, and extraordinary varieties of plants and animals. As an experiment, a remarkably diverse group of people are loaded onto a boat and sent to live on this island. These people possess every conceivable talent and skill to create very comfortable lives for themselves. Three things are asked of them: take care of your health; work together in harmony; replenish what you consume. For satisfying these three simple requirements, these people are guaranteed lives of peace and abundance.

Like this theoretical experiment, we on Earth had the same opportunity. Early in our history, the combination of our natural resources and our human skills and abilities offered us extraordinary opportunities that we were not yet wise enough to recognize. Instead, we became embroiled in power struggles over our different ethnicities, territories, and belief systems. We chose to address our differences—ones that in reality presented unlimited opportunities—as opposing principles in competition rather than as complementary ones that enhance each other. Self-centered tribes, regions, and nations alienated and made enemies of each other. No one worked for the common good. This transformed our elegant equation into countless tragedies.

We have each become like tiny islands with limited resources. We defend, rather than share, our unique qualities. As a consequence, few find contentment. It never seems to occur to us that our many needs are mutual and connected. We seem unable to comprehend the intrinsic value and infinite potential of our differences.

Primitive Beliefs

There is no spiritual cohesion. There never has been a common spiritual ground. Up until now, there never could have been. Diverse peoples have never been linked as we are today with our increasingly sophisticated information technologies. While there has been no universal spirituality, there have been pockets of primitive beliefs and belief systems that emerged on different parts of our planet at different times in our history. We have referred to these belief systems as religions. We have had and continue to have many religions. The effect of these unique creeds has not been to bring us together but to permanently separate us.

Often they begin as cults. As each belief system grows, it gains power and inclusiveness. At the core of each is typically a creation story, often a variation of an earlier story. Mystery and supernatural events such as divine revelation and miracles are central to each belief system. Each religion has its sacred places and rituals. All of it is contrived out of ideas that were popular at a particular time or built upon the evolution of former ideas. Stories grew from fiction to fact, developed into "religions" and declared themselves sacred. This development was precisely backwards; only out of an understanding first of what is truly sacred can a belief system follow and grow. Given the origins of religions it is not surprising that there is fierce competition between them that often results in horrendous bloodshed. Fortunately, with the passage of time, the validity of these belief systems is coming under ever-greater scrutiny.

The increasing complexity of our time and the magnitude of the problems that we face raise profound questions for ancient religions. Quickly growing and increasingly integrated populations further complicate our lives and compound our problems. Many people have begun to question these old religious belief systems and even the idea of religion in general. What is religion and what is its mission? Is it to dwell on, venerate, and interpret the past? Or is it to develop new beliefs based on current knowledge? Ones that will nurture and sustain us as we confront each other and the new realities in our increasingly interconnected and interdependent world? How can religions, so divided themselves, accomplish such tasks? Enlightened by the collective wisdom of our past, many of us are coming to realize that in order to survive, we must shed the superstitious religions that hinder our progress and find a universal belief system that can unite the world's communities.

It seems that the role of theologians is to forever study ancient texts and endlessly debate their interpretations. Most theologians are swept away by, absorbed in, and dependent upon the existing current of religious institutional inertia. Many are buffered by academic insulation. It is unlikely that many theologians would be bold enough, could risk, or would even want to introduce the new spiritual thinking that is needed.

There are further stubborn questions for our ailing religious institutions. How can religion end the frenzy of self-centeredness that everywhere afflicts individuals, groups, and nations? How can religion convince the powerful who have vested interests in the status quo that their attitudes and actions are not only unsustainable but also catastrophic and terminal to themselves and everyone else? How can religion diffuse historical rivalries and debilitating and ruinous conflicts between contemporary adversaries? And, since people rarely act until there is a crisis, how can religions prepare their faithful for impending disasters that could be overwhelming?

At this time, we are not lacking in religious institutions that could address these issues. High priests and priestesses are not in short supply. There is quite a varied menu of teachers and scriptures from which to choose. It is remarkable that so many of these religions claim exclusive possession of *divinely inspired and infallible truth*. Surely, they cannot all possess what each claims to be: the one and only truth. Even more remarkable is the public's general unwillingness or inability to acknowledge and question this obvious contradiction.

Many people are content to embrace a particular myth, adopt a creed, or fall under the spell of a charismatic personality. Some followers are prepared to do almost anything, including sacrificing their lives to satisfy the doctrines of their faith. Tragically, in the name of fervently held religious beliefs, some of these followers become fanatics and take the lives of fellow humans. It seems never to occur to them that what they do is more important than what they believe.

Much of this behavior is rooted in ignorance. Because we have a need to ease our miseries, calm our fears, band together to compete with other groups, and generally understand the cause and purpose of life, we are receptive to ideas that satisfy these needs. As a consequence, we are overwhelmed with opposing dogma and rituals as religions compete for followers, financial support, and power. The path that should have led to clarity instead has led to other cells in the spiritual prison block. A clear view of reality has been distorted by multiple religions, sects, schools, creeds, and cults. A true understanding of reality has been lost in needless complexities, theatrics, and exploitation.

We praise distant mythological deities as we exploit our neighbors. We dream of the "hereafter" as we destroy the "here." Convinced that we are the exceptions that will be saved in an afterlife, we ignore our responsibility for saving ourselves in this life. We are willing, even anxious, to take giant leaps of faith, but refuse to take even small steps toward sound reason and common sense. We elevate fictional stories of gods and creation, fabricated by ourselves, to the status of divinely inspired dogma, freeze them in texts, and upon these shaky foundations build and perpetuate religious institutions.

Some of us have begun to see this nonsense for what it is. Doctrines that were formed before the age of science and written by churchmen profoundly ignorant of their world no longer hold any appeal for growing numbers of better informed individuals. Mainline churches have begun to lose millions of members. Still, these antiquated religions live on, perpetuated by enormous institutional inertia. Swept away in this tidal wave, theologians and clergy are forever engaged in a litany of interpretation upon interpretation of word after word of ancient stories that were written creatively in the first place. When they are not involved in the interpretation of ancient texts, they are involved in interpreting each other's interpretations. Indeed, interpretation has become an industry unto itself.

As a consequence, fundamental and uncomplicated messages about proper human conduct and just human relationships have gotten muddled and diluted and have been rendered impotent. Religions have fragmented into multiple forms of expression. Those of us who have longed for clarity and direction have gotten increasingly alienated and confused. Consequently, brutal behavior, social violence, and environmental degradation continue to worsen. There exists no belief system to draw us together to eliminate our problems. A glaring irony is that our religious divisions account for a large share of our armed conflict. Through the years, many bloody wars, genocide, crusades, missionary atrocities, and persecutions have taken place in the name of religion. Intelligent people find these occurrences and their religious justifications to be repulsive.

Many otherwise intelligent people are reluctant to engage in open conversations on religion. We find it difficult to remain dispassionate and rational. Religious beliefs and ideas are life-long habits, coveted addictions. These are very personal and highly charged issues. When they are challenged, even politely, our responses are emotional and defensive. We are cautioned not to speak about religion. It is a shunned subject that everyone knows ignites easily.

Part III

The Solution

"No matter how exalted we think ourselves, all that we can know and become has a material basis obedient to the decipherable laws of physics and chemistry. And no matter how intellectually far above the remainder of life we lift ourselves, and however technically proficient we become, we will stay a biological species, biological in origin, and thence adapted in mind and body to the living world that cradled us."

—Edward O. Wilson, 1998 Phi Beta Kappa Oration,
Harvard University

CONTEXT, PERSPECTIVE, AND TIME FRAMES

COSMOLOGY

Noted in the front of this book is a favorite quote from a person named Rahel: "If you wish to astonish the whole world, tell the simple truth." His statement, however, begs the question(s). What *is* the simple truth? The simple truth about *what*? In my context, it is the simple truth about life. What makes life healthy? What sustains life? What in life is "sacred"? "Sacred" is a very unusual word. What could a word like this mean?

There is a phenomenon that I refer to as *the way of life* (natural law). If we honor the way of life, we prosper. If we violate it, we suffer needlessly. To explore, discover, and understand the way of life requires context, perspective, and time frames. For these, we will turn to three areas. First, we will review some of what we know about cosmology (the origin and structure of the universe). Second, we will turn to evolutionary biology. How long has this planet and life been here? How long have we been here? What has life been through to get this far? Third, we will look at the world of religion. Where have all these religions come from and why?

The Danish philosopher and theologian Soren Kierkegaard observed that "Searching for truth is like searching in a pitch dark room for a black cat that isn't there." Truth is elusive. But truth and elements of truth are discoverable. Truth is stubborn. Truth is tough. These things we call facts are stubborn things. Chief Justice Oliver Wendell Holmes observed that "Truth is tough. It will not break, like a bubble, at a touch; you may kick it around all day like a football, and it will be round and full at evening."

From cosmology, we know that every hour we travel in excess of an incredible 1,665,000 miles. How do we do that? It is as though we are on a spacecraft within a spacecraft within a spacecraft (at least). The first spacecraft on which we are passengers is our planet as it orbits the star we call our sun at a speed of 65,000 miles an hour. Our solar system is the second spacecraft. We are passengers on it as it orbits our galaxy, the Milky Way, at 600,000 miles per hour. The Milky Way, the third spacecraft on which we are traveling, is speeding along among other galaxies in excess of 1,000,000 miles per hour. This gives us a total in excess of 1,665,000 miles traveled every hour of our lives. It may be, and likely is, that we are on a fourth space-craft, our universe, as it travels among other uni-verses in a multiverse.

Our planet is 7,926 miles in diameter and 24,000 miles in circumference, yet, in volume, Earth is only 3 millionths the size of our sun. We exist in a solar system comprised of the sun, nine planets, 78 moons (Earth: 1, Mars: 2, Jupiter: 17, Saturn: 28, Uranus: 21, Neptune: 8, and Pluto: 1), more than 30,000 asteroids, and countless comets and meteoroids. Of the nine planets, four are known as the inner (and terrestrial) planets: Mer-cury (3,029 miles diameter), Venus (7,519 miles diameter), Earth, and Mars (4,223 miles diame-ter). The five outer planets, which represent 99 percent of the mass of all the planets, are Jupiter (89,000 miles diameter), Saturn (75,000 miles diameter), Uranus (32,000 miles diameter), Nep-tune (31,000 miles diameter), and tiny Pluto (1,423 miles diameter), which is smaller than our moon. The sun, in comparison, is so large (865,000 miles diameter) that it comprises 99.85% of the *total mass* of our solar system.

As our planet orbits the sun at 65,000 mph, simultaneously it turns, rotating on its axis, at 1,000 miles an hour. To rotate fully once, it takes what we call a day. As we orbit our sun, our moon, 238,857 miles away, orbits us every 27 days, 7 hours, and 43 minutes. Earth is about 93,000,000 miles from the sun. The closest planet to the sun, Mercury, is about 36,000,000 miles from it. To give you a sense of the size of our solar system, Pluto, the most distant planet, is 3,666,000,000 miles from the sun. The circuit that we orbit around the sun is 600 million miles. To orbit once, it takes what we call a year.

While all this is going on, our solar system orbits the Milky Way galaxy. Envision this: the sun and its planets, asteroids, meteoroids, and comets all orbit together at 600,000 miles per hour like a huge self-contained space station billions of miles in diameter.

How long does it take for us to orbit the Milky Way galaxy one time? Recall that it takes Earth a year to get around the sun at 65,000 miles an hour. In contrast, our solar system is traveling around the galaxy at 600,000 miles per hour. But even at that speed it takes 225 *million* years to orbit the Milky Way galaxy *one time*.

The Milky Way galaxy is huge. It contains more than 200 billion stars. The nearest to us of the 200 billion is a star by the name of Proxima Centauri. It is one of a three-star system that also includes Alpha and Beta Centauri, which tumble over each other while Proxima Centauri orbits them. To reach Proxima Centauri from our solar system, traveling at the speed of light, 186,000 miles per second (at that speed, we could fly around Earth seven times in one second!), requires four years and three months. That's to reach the *nearest* star of well over 200 billion.

Just how big is this galaxy? The Milky Way is 100,000 light-years wide. A light-year is the distance covered in a year traveling at the speed of light, 186,000 miles per second: 5,880 billion miles. Multiply that times 100,000 and you have the distance across our galaxy. There is another way, perhaps a little more comprehensible, to visualize something 100,000 light-years wide. If we started at one end of our galaxy and traveled across it at 186,000 miles a second (the speed of light) for every second of every minute of every hour of every day of every year for 100,000 years, we would reach the other end. It's *large*. The word "incomprehensible" comes to mind. As recently as the 1920s, we thought the Milky Way galaxy was the entire universe. This was the equivalent of thinking the earth was flat.

As large as our galaxy is, we now know it is only one of 100 billion galaxies in the observable universe. Why do we say the "observable universe?" We exist on one of the spiral arms of the Milky Way galaxy. The gas, dust, and other stars (approximately 200 billion) in our galaxy block our vision, preventing us from observing the rest of the universe. Even though we can actually observe 100 billion galaxies, we estimate that there exists a trillion galaxies in the known universe. Scientists are now pondering the probability that there are many more universes. The nearest large galaxy to us is Andromeda, which contains about 400 billion stars. To reach Andromeda from the Milky Way, we would have to travel at the speed of light, 186,000 miles per second, for 2,200,000 years.

Galaxies are organized into clusters and super clusters. The Milky Way, Andromeda, and more than thirty other galaxies exist in a cluster by the name of the Local Group. The Local Group is 10 million light-years wide and *sits on the edge* of a super cluster by the name of Virgo. Virgo is hundreds of millions of light-years wide. To cross it requires hundreds of millions of years of travel at 186,000 miles per second. It contains thousands of galaxies. However, in cosmic terms, thousands of galaxies is not a big deal. Remember, there are an estimated *trillion* galaxies in the known universe. This super cluster, Virgo, with all its galaxies, is being drawn at a speed in excess of a million miles an hour toward some unfathomable mass that some cosmologists refer to as The Great Attractor.

Let's review all of this briefly. In general terms, our universe consists of clusters and super clusters of galaxies. These galaxies contain billions of stars like our sun. Planets orbit some of these stars. Moons orbit some of these planets. We exist on a planet orbited by a moon. Our planet and its moon orbits a star, the sun, at 65,000 miles per hour. The sun, along with the rest of our solar system, orbits the Milky Way galaxy at 600,000 miles per hour. The Milky Way galaxy, with all its stars, planets, and moons, travels among other galaxies at speeds in excess of a million miles an hour. This is the incredible system in which we exist and of which our tiny planet is an infinitesimally small part, a mere speck on the blueprint of existence.

EARTH

Now, let us return to planet Earth and consider how long our planet has been here, when life first appeared, and when we humans arrived. To do that, we turn to radiometric dating and the fossil record (a trace of an organism of a past geologic age).

From radiometric dating (the rate of radioactive decay is constant over time), we know Earth has been here for about 4.56 billion years. According to the fossil record, life began about 800 million years later, or 3.8 billion years ago. This life was in the form of primitive single-cell microorganisms. It took more than 3 billion years before the first multicellular plants and animals appeared. That was about 670 million years ago.

About 520 million years ago the age of invertebrates and vertebrates began. This period lasted for about 320 million years. At the end of this age, which was about 3.6 billion years since the first single-cell microorganisms appeared, it yielded insects and the beginning of fish and reptiles. That took us to 200 million years ago, at which time the age of reptiles began and lasted for about 130 million years. This was the time of the dinosaurs. About 70 million years ago the first mammals appeared. This marked the beginning of the age of the mammals (species that feed their young from mammary glands). It's the age we are in now. We are but one of 4,400 species of mammals.

What about us? How long has modern man been here? It is thought that between five and eight million years ago the succession of species that gave rise to us separated from the succession that led to the apes. From a common ancestor, the apes moved off in one direction and we, the hominids or family of humans, moved off in another. It is thought that the first genus of the hominids was *Ardipithecus*. It was followed by *Australopithicus*, *Kenyanthropus*, and finally our genus, *Homo*, which showed up between 1.5 and 2 million years ago. These were not *Homo sapiens*, however, but *Homo rudolfensis*, the earliest known member of our genus. These beings were not what we consider to be modern humans. In between the emergence of *Homo rudolfensis* and the eventual arrival of *Homo sapiens* (us), were *Homo habilis*, *Homo ergaster*, *Homo erectus*, *Homo antecessor*, *Homo heidelbergensis*, and *Homo neanderthalensis*. It was in Africa, between 100,000 and 150,000 years ago, that modern humans, *Homo sapiens* (sensible humans), emerged. From there, we spread through Africa, into Europe and Asia, and to the rest of our world.

We went through various stages. We began as and remained hunter-gatherers for tens of thousands of years until about 12,000 years ago. At that time, with the domestication of plants and animals, our agrarian age began. We remained in that age until the late 1700s, when the Industrial Revolution began in England. By the mid 1800s, the Industrial Revolution spread to Belgium, Germany, France, and the United States. Eventually, it spread to all the industrial nations. By the middle of the 1900s we transitioned into a post-industrial high-technology age, which led directly to the information age that emerged in the latter part of the century. Through all these periods, our population continued to rise.

It took from the very beginning of the evolution of our species to the year 1900 for us to reach a population of 1.6 billion. Then something extraordinary happened. Something that will likely never again occur on this planet. From the year 1900 to 1960, our population jumped from 1.6 billion people to 3 billion. In sixty years, we nearly doubled the population that it took all of evolution to produce. Then, in the next *thirty-nine years*, we doubled that number again when we reached a population of 6 billion in 1999. *In a hundred years*, from 1900 to 2000, *we quadrupled our population*. We are presently adding approximately 80 million people a year to our global population.

If we take a survey of the attitudes and behavioral patterns of a representative sample of all these people on a particular subject or issue, do a statistical distribution with our data and plot the results on a graph, we typically come up with something that we refer to as a bell curve (normal curve). See figure 1.

The two areas adjacent to the mean in the center of the curve represent the normal range (highest frequency) of behavior. Off to the right and left are standard deviations from the normal range. Beyond these standard deviations are more extreme deviations from the normal range. What does all this mean? It means that whatever the issue, the people on one side of the curve will likely have very different views than those on the opposite side. This often results in opposition, conflict, and strife, up to and including wars. This bell curve is a remarkable phenomenon. It represents one of the greatest challenges in life: how to bridge our differences. This very predictable pattern contributes to, and, in fact, practically guarantees, life's multiple interpersonal problems, instability and uncertainty.

Further contributing to life's instability and uncertainty is the fickleness of nature (natural disasters

such as earthquakes, hurricanes, volcanoes, torna-
does, cyclones, forest fires, floods, and droughts).
Also contributing are a vast number of illnesses that
we contract and from which we suffer, and an
extraordinary array of accidents that occur regularly. In addition, because we have so many people
and are a young species that has been largely ignorant of the physical reality in which we exist (and
which enables us to exist) we have created an
interrelated web of life-threatening environmental
problems. We are depleting our resources: our

BELL CURVE (NORMAL CURVE)

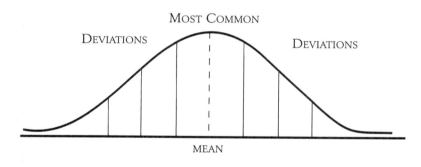

FIGURE 1

forests, fisheries, range lands, croplands, and plant
and animal species. We are destroying our own biological diversity. With advanced pumping tech-
niques, we are draining our aquifers and lowering
our water tables. We are polluting our air, water,
and soil. We are depleting the stratospheric ozone
that shields us from harmful ultraviolet radiation.

And, we are experiencing symptoms of global warming: heat waves, devastating droughts, dying forests, accelerated species extinction, melting glaciers, dying coral reefs, rising sea levels, and more frequent and intense storms.

This thing we call *life*, far from certain, is a fragile phenomenon. It is up and down like a seesaw and so are we. In our theatres, where we have for thousands of years told the stories of our lives, we have for symbols the classic masks of comedy and tragedy that portray joy and sorrow. Life has always been this way.

RELIGION

To explain life, we have turned to two disciplines that are almost diametrically opposed, science and religion. Science is very formal and rigid in the determination of its principles and theories. A scientific theory must survive a regimen of testing and re-testing by any observers and testers at any place and produce identical results time after time before it is accepted as fact. Science is almost perverse in its methodology of testing in attempts to get its theories to break. Yet, science is a very open process that welcomes and celebrates change when new discoveries are made.

Religion, on the other hand, is an untested collection of dogmatic principles. It is derived typically from supernatural sources and that which is referred to as "divine revelation." It's a phenomenon that was born when "priests" and "priestesses"

invented themselves, which they continue to do.
Religion does not like challenges or changes to its
dogma. The alteration of a few words of so-called
"revealed religion" can unravel and splinter religions into smaller groups. These in turn unravel
and splinter into even smaller groups. Christianity,
for example, has approximately thirty-three thou- 33,830
sand, eight hundred and thirty denominations.

Evidence of religion, art, and recorded events
dates back thirty to forty thousand years. There
have been an estimated one hundred thousand religions. Today we have ten thousand *distinct religions, of which 150 have one million or more
followers*. Some of the better known include Hin-
duism, which originated six thousand years ago;
Judaism, four thousand years ago; Buddhism (and
Confucianism and Taoism), twenty-six hundred
years ago; Christianity, two thousand years ago; and
Islam, fourteen hundred years ago.

We've worshipped everything from the sun, to
the moon, to Egyptian pharaohs and Roman emper-
ors. Then we created mythological gods in our own
image. Through our history, we've worshipped the
many gods of countless polytheistic religions. About
four thousand years ago, in the Middle East, someone came up with the idea that there is just one
God. This marked the beginning of the western
concept of monotheism (one God). That religion
was Judaism and the God Yahweh (misspelled
Jehovah in the King James Version of the Bible).

About fourteen hundred years later (twenty-six hundred years ago), Buddhism, Confucianism, and Taoism, all with *no gods*, emerged as powerful religious movements in the East.

In the last forty years of the first century A.D., in the approximate years 60 to 100 (no one knows for sure), long after the events that were claimed to have occurred, the New Testament gospels Mark, Matthew, Luke, and John were created decades apart. Theologians agree that the authors, whose identities are unknown, each with his or her own agenda and bias, created stories to match the prophecy of the Old Testament written two thousand years earlier. To embellish their stories, the writers employed the practice, common at the time, of incorporating fictional elements drawn from ancient writings of heroes and gods from pagan religions (today, we call this practice plagiarism).

In particular, they "borrowed" heavily from a rival and major religion in the Roman Empire, Mithraism, which had existed for at least seven hundred years. It originated in Persia, which is now Iran. Mithraism, based on a fictional character named Mithra, was popular in the first century with Roman soldiers and civil servants. The story line of Mithraism was strikingly similar to Christianity. Mithra was born of a virgin. At his birth were shepherds and magi kings. Kings were commonly inserted into these stories to represent royalty, signifying that the birth was important. Mithra's birth was celebrated on December 25, the same day the Christians adopted. In the tale of Mithra were miracle stories, resurrection, and ascension. The similarity in story lines made possible the easy conversion of Mithraism's followers to Christianity.

Out of all of this a new story was created (which learned theologians agree is largely fiction) and a new religion born—Christianity. With it came another god, "Christ," from the Greek word "Christos", an interpretation of the Hebrew word for messiah, or "mashiakh", meaning the anointed one (as prophesied in the Old Testament). At some point, someone declared that these contrived stories were the divinely inspired, infallible words of God. In other words, people were led to believe that the same god that they created in their stories was responsible for the stories they created.

About fourteen hundred years ago in Mecca, the leading city of Arabia, another prophet, Mohammed, appeared. He too heard and made note of the infallible words of God. His writings, which were recorded in small segments over a twenty-three-year period, were compiled in a book known as the Koran (Qur'an). Four-fifths the length of the New Testament, the Koran is considered by Muslims to be the final and infallible revelation of God's will. Born was another religion, Islam, and yet another god, Allah, meaning literally "The God." Not *a* god but *the* God. The one true God.

We have given these gods great powers. We say

these gods are omnipotent, meaning that they are all-powerful; omnipresent, meaning that they exist everywhere; and omniscient, meaning that they have all learning and knowledge. These stories have caused great worldwide confusion, conflict, and suffering. And wars. Sixty-six percent of our wars have been fought over these stories. *We kill each other over these stories.* It is the ultimate irony and a complete absurdity that we create these stories to establish examples of exemplary behavior and proper rules for living, then kill each other over them.

One does not have to be a genius to conclude that there is something absurd and fundamentally wrong here.

SACREDNESS:
A NEW UNDERSTANDING

INFANCY OF OUR INTELLIGENCE

When I was a child, my family attended church regularly. I served countless masses as an altar boy. It was my nature at a very young age, as it has been all my life, to be observant and contemplative. I observed the restrained and reverential behavior of people in church. They crossed themselves with "holy" water as they entered, bowed, genuflected, stood, kneeled, and prayed in reverent obedience. I also observed, curiously, that many of these same sanctimonious people were often irreverent, insensitive, and sometimes cruel outside of church. I sensed, instinctively, that there was something wrong. I did not yet know the word "hypocrisy."

As I continued to observe life, I was struck by how we seemed to complicate it unnecessarily. I thought to myself, "Life is not this complicated. Why do we make it more difficult than it is?" Wherever I went, as the years passed, I observed similar hypocritical and counterproductive behavioral patterns that I found disturbing.

I went on to live a very unusual life of many rich and diverse experiences in a variety of careers. Later in life, I studied at two of the world's most renowned divinity schools—Yale and Harvard. At the latter, I earned a master of divinity degree. I went to these schools to study ethics, issues associated with global ecological problems, and world religious belief systems. I went to continue on the learning track I had been on all my life. I was fifty years old the year I graduated from Harvard. As an older student, I remained objective in my study and analysis of world religions.

I studied all the major world religions. While they are all interesting and rich in history and rituals, one finds that they remain human constructs formed thousands of years ago in the infancy of our intelligence by people like you and me. The historical context and ancient mindsets that produced these belief systems are abundantly evident. Clearly they are all a part of our very early efforts to understand and cope with the withering and unrelenting demands of life. As such, they should be treated like all other institutions that we have created. Now, ancient and antiquated, these religions should be studied as history, not adopted as belief systems.

No disparagement or disrespect is meant by that statement. I appreciate the good efforts of all those who have preceded us honorably. We are no different from them in our quest for life's ultimate answers. Ghandi said it best when, with great candor, he observed that "Religious ideas are subject to the same laws of evolution that govern everything else in the universe." In other words, there comes a time to let go of dated ideas and advance as life demands just as we do in every other field of endeavor.

The study of religion, costly in time and funds, was a liberating and rewarding experience. It cleared my mind of the false religious dogma that as a child I was programmed—literally brainwashed (by the church)—to believe, just as children are today. That clearance was the second most valuable benefit I derived from my divinity school experience. The most valuable benefit was the discovery, on my own, of that for which I was searching. It happened like this:

With a cleared mind, I compared and contrasted our present circumstances with our ancient past. To paraphrase sociologist Lester Milbrath, over time we have developed an integrated and complex social, technical, and economic system so powerful that we can dominate and destroy each other and the rest of the natural world. Alongside it, we have retained an ethical system based on very old ideas. Ancient western religions, for example, would have us believe that a god exists as a monarch, rules over a kingdom, is distant from the world, relates primarily to humans, and saves whatever he chooses, thus relieving us of our responsibility for saving ourselves and other living things. Science, on the other hand, explains our physical world but provides no moral guidance for living within it. The lack of congruence between our major inherited religions and the power and exuberance of our modern world is gravely problematic. This is a reality that most of us choose to deny, or one of which we are unaware, and one that is perpetuated by clinging to ancient notions of what is sacred.

In a brilliant statement some twenty-six hundred years ago, the Buddha said, "To insist on a spiritual practice that served us in the past is to carry the raft on our back after we have crossed the river." Having crossed the river myself, so to speak, it was time for me to examine the concept of *sacredness*. A modern belief system must be based on a current understanding of what is sacred. But who is to say what is sacred, the scientist or the priest? Where does the truth lie?

In an article entitled "What Does it Mean to be Religious?" Dr. Clinton Lee Scott wrote, and I agree, that no one person or category of people has

the inside track on truth. Truth may be discovered
". . . by scientists, poets, prophets, housewives, and
garage mechanics. And always by the one way of
human experience. Truths are derived from the
experience of men and women living not apart
from the world (not cloistered away), but within
it, in all the temptations, problems, and perplexi-
ties of the daily round of human relations. It is in
this round of the common everyday life that to
many of us religion must have meaning, if it is to
have any meaning at all. Not in formal observances,
not in creeds or doctrines, however long ago pro-
claimed, but in the lives we live, in the home, in
the community, and in the world, is the religious
way of life to be found."

SPIRITUAL

Many of us say we do not like organized religion but that we are "spiritual." There is something about the word that feels right to us. But what does *spiritual* really mean? Our world has taken enormous liberties with this word. Religious groups engage in "holy wars" (now there's a play on words) where acts of terrorism are committed. A busload of innocent people, including children, is firebombed and those responsible claim to be *spiritually* motivated. Physicians are murdered over the very complex abortion issue and the killers explain that the murders are *spiritually* justified. If each person in a group were asked to define the word "spiritual," each one, and understandably so, would have a different definition. What does this word mean?

"Spiritual" may be defined as having to do with

sacred matters or *sacred* things. We have arrived at the word "sacred." It sounds wonderful. But what does it mean? "Sacred" may be defined as that which is associated with gods or that which is associated with religion. When we say that "sacred" is that which is associated with gods, the question arises immediately, "What and whose god or goddess are we talking about?" Most everyone seems to have different ideas about the concept of a god or gods. Seldom, and understandably so, is there agreement. If there is agreement on anything, it might be that life has its mysteries.

When we attempt to define or worship these mysteries, particularly as gods, invariably we create religious problems. Definitions are divisive and invite conflicts. Historically, we have had and to this day continue to have conflicts. Worship of these gods is diversionary and distracting. Our attention gets focused *out there* somewhere, worshipping *something* we have been programmed to believe exists, is sacred, and by which we are going to be "saved." We are going to be saved while at the same time we live horribly unhealthy lives, go to war with our neighbors literally and figuratively, and destroy our environment and deplete our resources. Yet, we are going to be saved. It doesn't make sense.

Another understanding of "sacred" is that which is associated with *religion*. We have gone from "spiritual," having to do with the sacred, to "sacred," having to do with religion. We haven't gotten very far. The obvious question is, "What is religion?" Religion may be defined as a belief in, or worship of, a god. That definition takes us back to gods. Immediately, the same problematic issues arise: What and whose god or goddess? The conflicts over definitions of gods. The diversion and distraction of our attention.

Religion may also be defined as a belief system having to do with the cause, purpose, and nature of the universe. In fact, this is what we have done since the beginning of conscious thought, and with very little knowledge. Early man created gods, creation stories, and religions to explain the cause, purpose, and nature of the universe.

Today, we do not need supernatural gods to explain these things. The generally accepted theory for the *cause* of the universe is the big bang theory. Since we understand only a very small portion of the universe, we don't have a clue as to its *purpose* or if it has a purpose. However, the *nature* of the universe is another matter. It is here where the enigma unravels. It is here where *sacredness* is revealed.

SACRED CONSTRUCT

Philosopher Arthur Schopenhauer noted that all truth passes through three stages. First, it is ridiculed. Second, it is violently opposed. Third, it is accepted as self-evident. Such a truth has emerged in our lifetime. It informs us that we exist as a tiny fragment of an immensely larger interlocking whole in which all of the parts are interconnected and dependent upon each other for survival. Allow me to repeat that. *A truth has emerged that informs us that we exist as a tiny fragment of an immensely larger interlocking whole in which all of the parts are interconnected and dependent upon each other for survival.* Simply put, everything is connected to everything else. We exist, not separately, but in communion with all living things. Life is an interrelated, interdependent phenomenon. Everything is in relationship. That is

Truth that has emerged

the nature of the universe. That is the nature of life.

"Everything is in relationship. So what," one might respond, and ask, "What is the practical value of *that* understanding?" It's a good question. The practical value lies in the realization that for us there are several relationships that are foundational. I refer to these as the *foundational relationships* of our lives. These are three relationships out of which all other relationships follow and occur. The first is our relationship with our *self*. The second is our relationship with *others*, and the third is our relationship with our *environment*. If we chose one word to summarize each of these relationships, our relationship with our self is about *health*, in all of its dimensions. Our relationship with others is about *kindness*. Our relationship with our environment is about *respect*.

FOUNDATIONAL RELATIONSHIPS

SELF . . . . .HEALTH
OTHERS . . . . .KINDNESS
ENVIRONMENT . . . . .RESPECT

The quality of our lives reflects the quality of these foundational relationships. This is a *sacred construct* that exists as an integral part of reality. This is not a human construct. Why do I say this is a sacred construct? Recall that our understanding of the word "sacred" is that which is associated with religion. Religion is a belief system that has to do with the nature of life. The nature of life is relational. These are the foundational relationships of our lives. Again, this is not a human construct. This is simply the way life works. This is not contrived or fictional. This is not arbitrary or subject to dismissal. Nor is this in any way negotiable. How we take care of ourselves, each other, and our environment determines not only the quality of our lives but whether we and our species will live or die. *These relationships are sacred*. They are the wellsprings of life. We emerge from these relationships. We are sustained by them. We are surrounded by the very sacredness that, historically, we have sought from afar.

This understanding of sacredness must be recognized and addressed as a dynamic reality. It's not unchanging and vested in the past like archaic dogma. We are continually refining our understanding of how to optimize these three foundational relationships—how to better care for ourselves, relate to each other, and care for our environment. It is as Greek philosopher Heraclitus observed, "You cannot step into the same river twice." Why is that? It is because the river is forever flowing and changing. Yet, it remains the same river. Similarly, our understanding of what optimizes these relationships flows out of a stream of knowledge that continually changes. These foundational relationships will always exist. Our understanding of how to optimize them evolves as our knowledge grows.

The spirit (from the Latin *spiritus* for *breath*) that animates life exists in, expresses itself through, and is sustained by these foundational relationships. If we destroy any of these relationships (our health, our relationships with each other and our environment), there we extinguish the spirit (the breath) of life. There is no place left through which the phenomenon that we call *life* can express itself (can breathe). The vitality is gone as it is in a person without breath. *To live a spiritual life (to breathe) is to honor these three basic relationships in all their manifestations.*

This is the much sought after key to the concept of *sustainability*: the understanding that we must leave this planet as we found it or improve it so those generations that follow us will have the same opportunities we have enjoyed. This is an awesome challenge given that we add approximately 80 million people a year to our planet. That is an addition of approximately 1,538,000 people *each week* to feed, clothe, house, educate, employ, transport, govern, protect, and keep healthy. The key to sustainability is to take the word apart and make two words of it: *sustain ability*, i.e., *our ability to sustain* these three foundational relationships: our health, our relationships with others, and the health of our environment. How do we do this?

We do this by identifying our responsibilities. So often we ask, "What is the purpose or the meaning of life?" These are questions that send us only in circles. The appropriate question is, "What are the *responsibilities* of life?" The answer again lies in taking the word apart and making two words of it: *response abilities*. We must develop our *abilities to respond* to life's challenges and stimuli so as to optimize and sustain our foundational relationships.

This understanding of sacredness does not mandate worship but responsibility. Right living is about behavior, not worship. Salvation (saving ourselves from harm or loss) is not delivered, it is earned by ourselves. The forgiveness of our "sins" lies not in the hands of some external god; it lies in our alignment with the uncompromising demands of the reality in which we exist. At this time in our evolution, *this understanding of sacredness is easily within our perception and grasp.*

CRITICAL MIND SHIFT

In his book, *Religions of the World*, Houston Smith writes of the two issues on which most religions agree. They all advise adherence to some version of the Golden Rule and avoidance of self-centeredness. Generally, we do neither one. Self-centered and shameless, we too often do to others and our environment whatever we can get away with. We get by with this behavior in the short term. In time, however, we find that we are victims of our own exploitation. For life reveals an exquisite intimacy among all phenomena.

Life also broadcasts a riveting truth from which there is no escape. I refer to it as the reverse side of the Golden Rule. Whereas the Golden Rule suggests that we do to others as we would have others do to us, the "reverse side" of the Golden Rule does not suggest anything but warns that *what we*

do to others we do to ourselves. In an interconnected world, all exploitation and oppression
inevitably returns to its source. This is a reality that
we must understand, and from this understanding
make the critical mind shift required of us if we are
to sustain our species and advance our civilization.
This mind shift is to understand clearly, unequivo-
cally, that *what we do to others we do to ourselves*.
What does this mean? The answer is evident in our
foundational relationships. In each there exists a
dynamic between self and other.

Consider our relationship with our environment. If we damage and destroy our environment,
we damage and destroy ourselves. In our relationships with other people, if we mistreat and are
unkind to others, our actions will return to haunt
and torment us in one form or another over time. In
our relationship with ourselves, if we abuse ourselves (our health) in any one of countless ways,
sooner or later, we will suffer the consequences.
When all of this becomes evident and acted upon,
our belief system (religion) and our behavior
become fused. Our belief system is not just something for one day of the week, or a particular time
of the day when we pray or bow to this or that god,
or to be celebrated in special places only. Our belief
system becomes our lifestyle, and our lifestyle
becomes aligned with and honors the larger reality
in which we exist.

Often we are confronted by well-meaning people

who read, quote from, or thump their "holy" books. They are everywhere: on television, radio, newspapers, magazines, and billboards. They even knock on our doors to evangelize and proselytize. In interacting with these people it often becomes evident that they don't know how to take of care of their health, how to get along with their neighbors, or understand our fragile relationship with our environment. One feels like saying to them, "What you have in your book is fine but what is going on in the rest of your life?" It's like walking down an aisle in a supermarket and seeing a sign in one section that reads "Health Foods." We think to ourselves, "If these are the health foods, what's going on in the rest of the store?"

Many of us have been taught that a creator has "endowed" us with something called "free will." This ingenious bit of theological inventiveness, among so many others, relieves gods of the responsibility for having created the dark side of life. Gods get the credit for all the good things and we, because of "free will," get the blame for all the bad, which is very clever. That aside, do we *really* have free will? Yes, of course. We can do whatever we like. We can lead unhealthy lifestyles. We can mistreat and exploit others. We can pollute our air, water, and soil and deplete and destroy our resources. In other words, we can and do destroy the foundational relationships of our lives. We have

free will. But *we do not have free will over the con-*

sequences. We cannot will the consequences. In an interrelated, interdependent world, the consequences are fixed. Our only choice is to either *honor the way of life and prosper or violate the way of life and suffer, needlessly.*

Sacredness is not a complex and difficult issue to understand. It is found in real life relationships here and now, not out there somewhere. Sacredness is not about a Supreme Being. It's about a *way of being.* The focus of our beliefs must shift from what was imagined to exist and be sacred in some heavenly realm to what *does* exist and *is* sacred here and now. It is time to find our comfort not in the worship of distant mythological gods, but in present, real-life relationships with each other, with our extraordinary environment, and with our own unique individuality.

These "commandments" are not issued by a god, but by the undeniable reality of our existence. Certainly the traditional "Gods" of some of our historical religions would approve of this shift of emphasis. When we take care of ourselves and each other, and leave our environment as we found it or improve it, we are living a sacred life. One would think that if there exists anything benevolent in dimensions beyond our perception—call it a god, creator, supreme being, the force, universal intelligence, or divine consciousness—that it, she, him, or them would cheer us wildly when the focus of our lives is on health for ourselves, kindness toward each other, and respect for our environment. For what more could any god of any belief system anywhere ask of us?

THREE SIMPLE RULES

Many of us are familiar with the Ten Commandments that appear in Exodus, the second book of the Bible, written some thirty-three hundred years ago. What do these commandments say? The first four have to do with a god and the Sabbath. The remaining six are about behavior. We are told to honor our parents and to not murder, steal, lie, commit adultery, or covet.

We would all agree that we have learned a few things in the last thirty-three hundred years. It may be that instead of the Ten Commandments, we require just three simple rules for living that say and do more than these ten. If we followed these three simple rules—*seven words*—we would eliminate the majority of problems and suffering in our world (problems that the Ten Commandments don't even address). It's of interest to note that none of these three rules appear in the Ten Commandments.

The first is *be healthy*. We are, each of us, like a cell in the body of the human species. The health of all of us taken together determines the health of our species and civilization. These bodies and minds in which we live may be the most exquisite "machines" on the planet. We abuse them in ways we wouldn't dream of doing to our material possessions like our cars, computers, or our homes. Yet, our bodies and minds are our homes. Perhaps the reason that we don't value them more is that we get them for free. We are given these most prized possessions at birth. By the time we realize their value, for many of us, it is very late if not too late. *Be healthy*. When we are, it is easier to follow the second simple rule.

The second rule is: *Be kind*. The Ten Commandments instruct us to honor our parents, which is fine. Aside from that they tell us not *what to do* but *what not to do*: thou shall not murder, steal, lie, commit adultery, or covet. In all our relationships, *what we need to do* is simply to be kind. We need to treat each other, our friends and neighbors, better. We must stop exploiting each other. It doesn't matter how much money we have or earn, what size house we live in, what kind of car we drive, how many academic degrees we may have accumulated, what accomplishments we may have achieved, or what our title or position is. Nor does it matter what our gender, race, religion, age, national origin, sexual orientation, or political affiliation is. *What matters* is whether or not we are kind to one another.

The third simple rule is: *Respect the environment*. In every conceivable way, we are linked to our environment. We evolved from it. Everything comes from our environment. If we destroy our environment, we destroy ourselves. It's that simple.

Three rules, seven words. If we follow them, our lives will change. As many of our lives change our world begins to change. *Be healthy. Be kind. Respect the environment*. If you wish to astonish the whole world, tell people that—the simple truth.

THE FOUNDATIONAL
RELATIONSHIPS

THE LAW OF ONE

Many of us are ready for a belief system that actually promotes harmony. It is apparent that we live in a world where we are destructive to ourselves, each other, and the ecological systems that enable us to exist. The belief system I describe emerges from the awareness and comprehension of the oneness in which we exist and the sacredness of the relationships by which it is sustained. The unwritten *Law of One* informs us that all that exists is a part of and is affected by everything else that exists.

This "law" acknowledges and honors the dynamic equilibrium among all life forms. It recognizes the existence of universal principles: *oneness, diversity, interrelatedness, individuality, and interdependence.*

Universal Principles

Oneness: All that exists is a part of and is affected by everything else that exists.

Diversity: The whole is comprised of an infinite number of diverse parts.

Interrelatedness: All parts are interrelated.

Individuality: All parts are unique.

Interdependence: All parts depend upon each other for survival.

These principles confirm that our reality is a product of an infinite number of diverse and unique interrelated and interdependent parts. An understanding of these principles yields virtues such as *reverence* for the oneness of which we are a part, *universal benevolence and kindness* toward each other, and *industry*. We understand that in order to live we must be industrious. In doing so, we take from the oneness but understand our responsibility to replenish and make it whole again. In other words, we borrow instead of take.

This understanding changes forever the way we think about and conduct our relationships with ourselves, with each other, and with our environment. It explains how we have created our problems and provides clear direction on how we can change. It's a system that calls for individual responsibility and initiative.

Within this realm of understanding lie the

treasures we are able to discover if we are wise enough to open ourselves to the possibilities of our age. These are treasures in the fullest sense. In their discovery lies the fate of humankind and many other species.

The simple truth is the way of life as it really is. It is reality, not myth or superstition. If we honor it, we prosper. If we violate it, we suffer and condemn our future to calamity. All of life is about relationships. As I have written, the foundational relationships of life are with self, with others, and with our environment. Everything else follows. We complicate life unnecessarily. We need simply to be healthy, be kind, and respect our environment.

"Be healthy, be kind, and respect our environment" is not enough for some people. They want specific instructions. Fortunately, knowledgeable people have amassed a great amount of information about how to care for ourselves, relate to others, and respect our environment. This information is updated constantly. Moreover, due to the high-tech information age in which we exist, the information is widespread and available. We need only to access and incorporate it into our lives. As an introduction, let me offer the following about each of our foundational relationships.

Relationship with Self

In a word, our relationship with ourselves is about *health* in all its mental and physical dimensions. The health and well-being of each of us as individuals and collectively as organizations determines the vitality of our civilization and of our planet. We are each a cell of the body we call the human species. We can be neither more nor less than what we make of ourselves.

We are wrong to complain about conditions in our world and to feel that we are unable to make a difference for better or worse. We must always question ourselves. What do we do to develop our abilities and potential? Do we educate ourselves about our health and the health of our planet? Are our habits constructive? Are we healthy in mind and body? How do we treat others? Are we kind? How do we treat ourselves? Do we have the courage to honor ourselves and become the best we can be? "The tragedy in life for most of us," noted Erich Fromm, "is that we die before we are born." By this he meant that we die before we are born into our unique potential.

Until we have fulfilled our responsibility to develop ourselves, we cannot critique the world without acknowledging our own destructive habits. By what we know and do, we make a difference. Each of us is a change agent. Individually, we can abuse ourselves in whatever manner we choose until finally we succumb. Conversely, we can be healthy and whole. Life cannot be violated beyond a critical point before its systems begin to fail. Each of us is the person over which we have the most control and the one easiest to change. When the errors of our ways shout at us, it is absurd for us to allow them to enjoy repetition. We must recognize and correct our errors. In so doing, others learn by our example.

RELATIONSHIP WITH OTHERS

In a word, our relationship with others is about *kindness*. Too often, we act only in our perceived self-interest. We feel that if we do not look out for ourselves, who will? In an interrelated world, we are obliged also to look beyond ourselves. In the Talmud, Rabbi Hillel wrote, "If I am not for myself who will be? But if I am for myself only, what am I?" In an interdependent existence, we ignore and mistreat others at our peril. We are like links in a chain. The fate of each link affects the fortune of all others.

There is individuality but not independence. To think differently is to delude ourselves. We are dependent upon each other at every turn. Our integrity affects the integrity of the whole.

We are each a part of a system of relationships that embrace our family, friends, neighbors, business associates, organizations, communities, nations, and family of nations. No single object or entity exists independently. Within this pattern of existence, destructive conduct, clearly nonsensical, returns to us in one form or another.

When we think only of ourselves, we invite conflict and everyone involved suffers. *What we do to others, we do to ourselves.* Those of us aware of this have begun altering our lives to conform to principles and virtues that nurture and sustain relationships. As we replace our destructive habits with ones that are constructive, everyone profits.

Relationship with
Our Environment

In a word, our relationship with our environment is about *respect*. We live on a planet soaring through space. We call this spacecraft Earth. It is a spacecraft (Earth) within a spacecraft (solar system) within a spacecraft (Milky Way galaxy), as I've explained earlier.

We are a product of this tiny orb that is our world. Over billions of years, we have evolved in concert with other species of plants and animals. As a part of this whole, we, like all living things, are subject to the natural laws that enable everything to exist. Every physical thing we require and enjoy is derived from our world. Everything. Every breath we breathe, every drop we drink, and every bite of food we eat is derived from our environment. Every bit of clothing, medicine, building material, and everything else is drawn from this same source. This world gave birth to us and countless other species of plants and animals. Now much of life, including our own, is threatened. We are polluting and decimating life-support systems, plundering resources, and driving species to extinction.

It is a great irony. We search the cosmos for evidence of the presence of even the most primitive form of life. Here, on earth, we destroy whole ecosystems and habitats that teem with all manner of extraordinary life forms.

The rate and range of global environmental deterioration is unprecedented. It is driven by the relentless needs of a global population growing out of control. Parasite-like and swarming, we are destroying our environment. With astonishing speed, we are attacking our ecosystems like businesses in liquidation. We have upset an extraordinary array of life that took billions of years and endless experiments to produce.

Environmental problems cross the boundaries of nation states, political and cultural ideologies, academic disciplines, business interests, and religious theologies. They affect the affluent and the impoverished, developed and developing nations, individuals and whole societies. These problems are far more than just another on a list of major concerns. *This* foundational relationship with the environment is at the core of our existence. Our relationships with these ecosystems are sacred. Nowhere do we find clearer evidence that *what we do to others, we do to ourselves* than in our relationship with our biosphere (Earth and its atmosphere where life exists).

Opportunity and Responsibility

In summary, we must understand that these three foundational relationships are sacred. They must be honored. To do so is not easy. In the economy and culture in which we live, great attention and diligence are required to remain healthy, be kind, and not harm our environment. There are many among us who do not hold these as high priorities for a variety of reasons, largely because of ignorance. Perhaps that is why we need to organize ourselves around a set of universal beliefs that we hold to be sacred. We all require constant reminders. We need to be kept current. We need the support of each other.

We are a young species not unlike a child finding its way. If we make the right choices based upon our current and expanding knowledge, we will succeed and advance our civilization. If, instead, we ignore what we know and insist upon violating the reality that enables us to live, we will suffer grave costs. Sacredness is like an orchard. Those who understand and respect the non-negotiable rules of life nurture the trees and enjoy the fruit. Those who don't understand or ignore the rules of life destoy the trees one by one until there is no more orchard and no more fruit.

We have an opportunity and a responsibility to correct an innocent error that began thousands of years ago in the infancy of our intelligence. We did not then understand what is truly sacred. Instead of recognizing the sacredness in life all around us, we created and worshipped mythological gods.

We created these fictional supernatural beings to explain the mysteries of life and to provide us with the courage to face life's challenges and tragedies. Over time, we transformed fiction into fact and forfeited our power to these deities. We then wove a web of deceit to respond to every logical challenge to our own contrived stories. With the knowledge we have today, it is long past time to let go of these ancient stories and shift our emphasis to that which is clearly sacred here and now. We have everything we require on this spaceship we call Earth to create a splendid world and fulfilling lives for ourselves. To do so means to be responsible for our health, to be kind to others, and to respect our environment. That's the simple truth.

ABOUT THE AUTHOR

Joseph R. Simonetta holds a master of architecture degree from the University of Colorado. He also studied architecture at the University of Southern California. He holds a master of divinity degree from Harvard Divinity School, and he also studied at Yale Divinity School. He holds a B.S. in business from Penn State University.

Born November 22, 1943 in a World War II housing project in Bethlehem, Pennsylvania, he was the second of three sons of an immigrant blue-collar steelworker and his wife. He was raised in the shadows of the blast furnaces of the Bethlehem Steel Corporation. He has since lived for significant amounts of time in California, Colorado,

Massachusetts, Connecticut, Florida, Greece, and New Zealand.

His rich life experiences encompass many fields. He has been an Army officer, a professional athlete, a computer programmer, an entrepreneur and businessman, an architectural designer, an environmental activist, an author, twice a nominee for Congress, and a nominee for president. This book is based on his lecture series, "Astonish the World, Tell the Simple Truth."

WALSCH BOOKS is an imprint of Hampton Roads Publishing Company, edited by Neale Donald Walsch and Nancy Fleming-Walsch. Our shared vision is to publish quality books that enhance and further the central messages of the *Conversations with God* series, in both fiction and non-fiction genres, and to provide another avenue through which the healing truths of the great wisdom traditions may be expressed in clear and accessible terms.

Hampton Roads Publishing Company

. . . for the evolving human spirit

Hampton Roads Publishing Company
publishes books on a variety of subjects including
metaphysics, health, complementary medicine,
visionary fiction, and other related topics.

For a copy of our latest catalog,
call toll-free, 800-766-8009,
or send your name and address to:

Hampton Roads Publishing Company, Inc.
1125 Stoney Ridge Road
Charlottesville, VA 22902
e-mail: hrpc@hrpub.com
www.hrpub.com